Revised Edition

# Tom Brady

By Jeff Savage

AMAZING ATHLETES

Lerner Publications Company • Minneapolis

*For Bailey Savage—as cool as Tom Brady*

Lerner Publications Company
A division of Lerner Publishing Group, Inc.
241 First Avenue North
Minneapolis, MN 55401 USA

For reading levels and more information, look up this title at www.lernerbooks.com.


Library of Congress Cataloging-in-Publication Data

Savage, Jeff, 1961-
    Tom Brady / by Jeff Savage. — 2nd revised edition.
        pages cm. — (Amazing athletes)
    Includes index.
    ISBN 978–1–4677–4582–6 (pbk. : alk. paper)
    ISBN 978–1–4677–4590–1 (eBook)
    1. Brady, Tom, 1977—Juvenile literature. 2. Football players—United States—Biography—Juvenile literature.  I. Title.
    GV939.B685S38 2015
    796.332092—dc23 [B]                                                     2014008796

Manufactured in the United States of America
1 – BP – 7/15/14

# TABLE OF CONTENTS

Wet Win                             4

Learning to Compete                11

Waiting His Turn                   14

Seizing the Moment                 18

Keep on Winning                    23

Selected Career Highlights         29
Glossary                           30
Further Reading & Websites         31
Index                              32

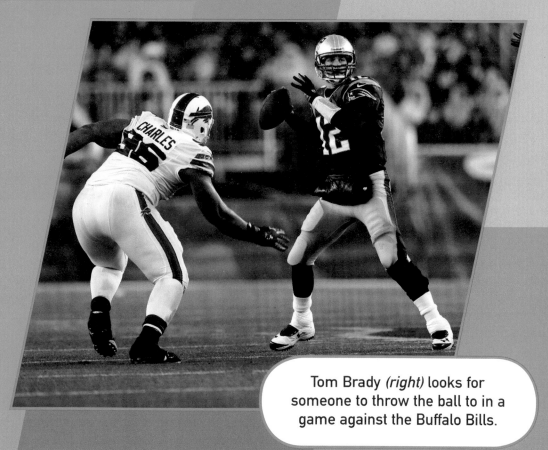

Tom Brady *(right)* looks for someone to throw the ball to in a game against the Buffalo Bills.

# WET WIN

New England Patriots **quarterback** Tom Brady ran onto the field. Water pelted his helmet. The crowd at Gillette Stadium in Foxborough, Massachusetts, roared under its rain gear.

Tom and the Patriots were playing the

Buffalo Bills on December 29, 2013. It was the last game of the **regular season**. If New England won, they would finish with the second-best record in their **conference**. The Patriots led at halftime, 16–3.

New England had the ball to start the second half. But they were in a tough spot. It was third down. They needed 32 yards to reach a first down. Instead of going for the first down, they decided to try to trick the Bills.

Tom holds onto a slippery ball as he runs down the field in the rain.

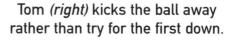

Tom *(right)* kicks the ball away rather than try for the first down.

Tom took the **snap**. Then he kicked the ball. The **punt** sailed 32 yards down the field.

Buffalo hadn't expected the punt on third down. But Tom wasn't pleased with the result.

"It could have been a lot better," he said. Quarterbacks rarely punt.

The Bills scored a touchdown to make the score 16–10. They sent the **kickoff** high and deep.

New England **running back** LeGarrette Blount caught the ball. He stormed up the field. It looked like Blount was going to score! But Buffalo caught up to him at their own 20-yard line.

Tom tossed a sharp pass to teammate Shane Vereen a few plays later. Touchdown! Both teams would score again, but New England's lead was too much for Buffalo to overcome. The Patriots won the game, 27–17.

Tom *(right)* celebrates with a teammate after another Patriots' touchdown.

Tom *(center)* talks with coach Bill Belichick *(right)* during the game.

Tom didn't feel much like celebrating after the game. He knows the regular season is just the beginning. Winning the Super Bowl is the ultimate goal. "We put together a great season, but it doesn't matter much now," he said.

Tom is one of the most successful quarterbacks in the history of the National Football League (NFL). He has won three Super Bowl titles with the Patriots. He was named Most Valuable Player (MVP) of the Super Bowl twice. Could Tom and his teammates get to the big game again?

The Patriots have been to the Super Bowl seven times. Only the Dallas Cowboys and the Pittsburgh Steelers have played in the Super Bowl more times.

Tom grew up near San Francisco in the 1980s. At that time, San Francisco quarterback Joe Montana *(above)* was at the top of his game.

# LEARNING TO COMPETE

Tom was born August 3, 1977. He was the fourth child of Galynn and Tom Brady Sr. The Bradys lived in San Mateo, a city near San Francisco, California. Tom was the baby brother to three sisters—Maureen, Julie, and Nancy. The entire family was crazy about sports.

Tom's boyhood hero was Joe Montana. During the 1980s, Montana was the Super Bowl-winning quarterback of the San Francisco 49ers. Just like Montana, Tom was not especially big or fast. But he loved to play sports. By the age of six, Tom was challenging older boys to run races.

Tom hated to lose. And sometimes he was not a good sport about losing. He threw his video game controller at the TV. He smashed his tennis racket on the court. "It got to where nobody wanted to play with me," he said.

In 1991, when Tom was fourteen, he started going to Junipero Serra High School. By this time, he'd learned to control his emotions. Serra High was known for its sports programs. Tom played catcher on the school's baseball team. But football was Tom's favorite sport.

Tom *(left)* stretches to tag out a player during a baseball game at Serra High.

In addition to daily practice, Tom created a tough workout program to stay in shape. Tom threw for nearly 4,000 yards and 31 touchdowns during high school. His skills drew the attention of more than 75 colleges around the country.

Tom was a talented baseball player. The Montreal Expos picked him in the 1995 baseball draft. But Tom chose to go to college and play football.

# WAITING HIS TURN

In 1995, at the age of 17, Tom sorted through his **scholarship** offers. He chose the University of Michigan, whose team name is the Wolverines. He moved away from home and became Michigan's **third-string** quarterback. College was fun for Tom, but he didn't get to play his first two years. He grew frustrated.

"I turned into a whiner," Tom admitted. He told his coach, Lloyd Carr, that he wanted to transfer to the University of California. Coach Carr convinced Tom not to give up. "Just put everything else out of your mind and worry about making yourself better," he told his young player.

Tom did as his coach told him. In 1998, in his third year, he became the team's starting quarterback. Over the next two years, Tom guided the Wolverines to a record of 20 wins and five losses. Tom's final college pass was a game-winning touchdown. It earned the Wolverines a dramatic 35–34 win over the University of Alabama in the Orange Bowl.

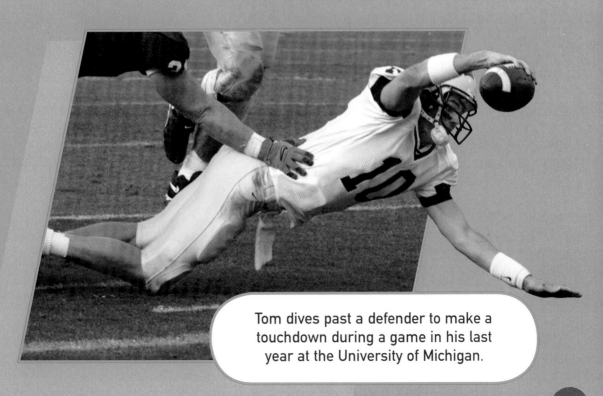

Tom dives past a defender to make a touchdown during a game in his last year at the University of Michigan.

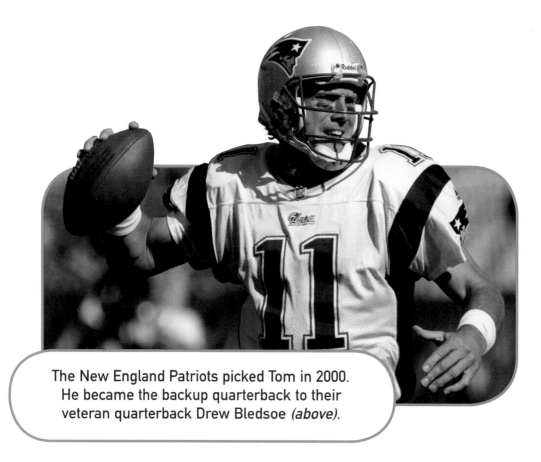

The New England Patriots picked Tom in 2000. He became the backup quarterback to their veteran quarterback Drew Bledsoe *(above)*.

But during the 2000 National Football League (NFL) **Draft**, coaches were not impressed. Tom wasn't drafted until the New England Patriots took him in the sixth round. He was very disappointed.

He joined the New England Patriots as a **rookie** quarterback. He would back up the team's **veteran** quarterback Drew Bledsoe.

In the 2000 season, Tom watched the Patriots finish last in their **division**. For the year, he completed just one pass for six yards. But Tom didn't pout. Instead, he worked harder. He practiced his footwork and memorized the team's **playbook**.

The 2001 season began badly. The Patriots lost their first two games. During the second loss, Bledsoe suffered a serious chest injury. He would be out for the season. Coach Belichick told Tom he was going to start the third game.

Patriots' head coach Bill Belichick noticed that Tom squeezed the ball with a hard grip. This grip allowed him to throw a tight spiral. But this way of throwing also meant he didn't throw the ball very far. Tight spirals tend to be more on target. Tom liked being an accurate passer rather than a long passer.

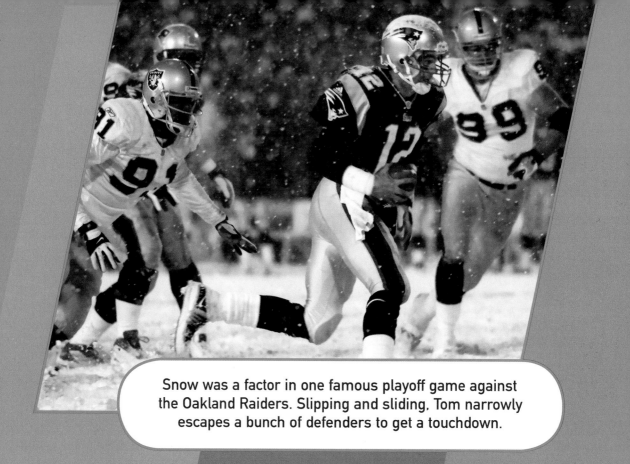

Snow was a factor in one famous playoff game against the Oakland Raiders. Slipping and sliding, Tom narrowly escapes a bunch of defenders to get a touchdown.

# SEIZING THE MOMENT

Tom seized the chance. He was careful and smart. In fact, he didn't throw an interception in his first 162 pass attempts. This was an NFL record. He led the Patriots to 11 wins in 14 games and into the **playoffs**.

In the first playoff game, New England played the Oakland Raiders at the Patriots' stadium in Foxborough, Massachusetts. It was January 2002, and snow blanketed the field. Playing was tough. At the end of the fourth quarter, the Patriots tied the game with a field goal. The game went into **overtime**. Tom marched his team close enough for the kicker to make another field goal and win the game.

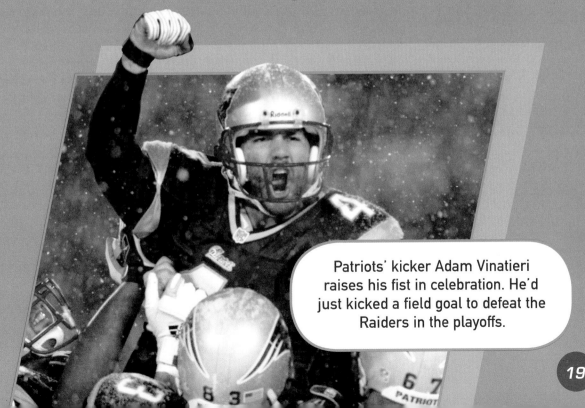

Patriots' kicker Adam Vinatieri raises his fist in celebration. He'd just kicked a field goal to defeat the Raiders in the playoffs.

A week later, the Patriots upset the Pittsburgh Steelers to reach the Super Bowl. Everyone was asking, who is this kid Tom Brady?

The Patriots weren't favored to win the Super Bowl. They'd be playing the high-powered St. Louis Rams.

Before playing in the Super Bowl in 2002, some of Tom's teammates paced the locker room. Others studied the game plan. What was Tom doing? He was stretched out on the floor taking a nap!

One by one, the Rams' major players ran onto the field. The Patriots came out in one big group—as a team. This was the way they wanted to play.

Tom kept his cool in the game. The Patriots carried a 17–3 lead into the fourth quarter. But the Rams stormed back to tie the game.

Tom gets out of trouble during Super Bowl XXXVI against the St. Louis Rams.

The Patriots had no timeouts left. Only 1:21 was left on the clock. Tom dodged defenders and completed a pass. Then he completed another. Calmly, he hurried his team. With three more passes, he moved the Patriots to the Rams' 30-yard line.

With seven seconds left on the clock, Adam Vinatieri *(left)* came through with a 48-yard field goal. Tom was the youngest quarterback to win a Super Bowl. He was also the youngest MVP.

Seven seconds remained. Vinatieri lined up for a field goal. The ball sailed through the uprights for a stunning victory! Tom was named the game's most valuable player (MVP). "Incredible," said Tom. "That's why you keep working hard."

Tom *(top right)* rides with his mother, Galynn *(center)*, and Mickey Mouse during a 2002 Disney World parade in Tom's honor.

# KEEP ON WINNING

Tom's life changed suddenly. As the Super Bowl MVP, he was the guest of honor at Disney World. Then he went to Boston, Massachusetts, for the team's victory parade. After that, he flew to Hawaii to play in the **Pro Bowl**.

The Patriots traded Bledsoe to Buffalo. New England became Tom's team. They finished the 2002 season with a record of 9–7 and missed the playoffs. In 2003, the Patriots lost the first game of the season to Buffalo, 31–0. Then New England won 17 of their next 18 games. They ended the season with their second Super Bowl victory in three years.

Tom *(right)* hands the ball to a running back during the Super Bowl on February 1, 2004.

New England kept up their winning pace in the 2004 season. They beat the Indianapolis Colts and the Pittsburgh Steelers in the playoffs. Then they went on to win their

Tom raises his arms after a Patriots touchdown in the Super Bowl.

third Super Bowl in four years. They beat the Philadelphia Eagles, 24–21.

The team kept on winning. But they didn't get back to the Super Bowl in 2005 or 2006. In 2007, the Patriots were 8–0 at midseason. They continued to win in the second half.

Tom married fashion model Gisele Bündchen in 2009.

Tom and his wife, Gisele Bündchen, pose for a photo.

Their last regular season win over the New York Giants gave them a perfect 16–0 season.

Tom and New England won two playoff games to reach the Super Bowl. They faced the Giants again. The game was tight throughout. In the end, New York pulled out the win, 17–14.

With Tom at quarterback, the Patriots are one of the best teams in the NFL every year.

They won no fewer than 10 games each season between 2008 and 2011. In 2012, New England advanced to the Super Bowl again. It was Tom's fifth time playing in the big game. Once again, they faced the Giants, and once again, the Giants won the game.

Tom (*center, with ball*) dodges New York Giants players in the Super Bowl on February 5, 2012.

After beating the Bills to end the 2013 season, New England fell to Peyton Manning and the Denver Broncos in the playoffs a few weeks later. But Tom has always been able to quickly get over losses and focus on the next game. That quality is one of the things that make him great. "I don't care about two years ago," he said. "I don't care about last year. The only thing I care about is this week."

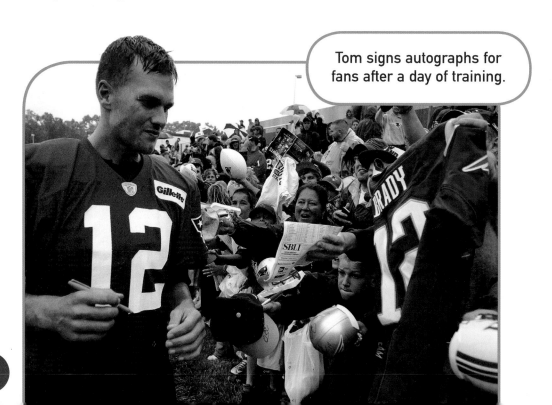

Tom signs autographs for fans after a day of training.

# Selected Career Highlights

**2013** Named to the Pro Bowl for the ninth time

**2012** Named to the Pro Bowl for the eighth time

**2011** Named to the Pro Bowl for the seventh
time

**2010** Named to the Pro Bowl for the sixth time
Named league MVP for the second time
Led NFL quarterbacks with 36
touchdown passes

**2009** Named to the Pro Bowl for the fifth time
Named NFL Comeback Player of the Year

**2008** Missed most of the season with a
knee injury

**2007** Led the Patriots to a perfect regular season record (16–0)
Named league MVP
Led NFL quarterbacks with 50 touchdown passes
Named to the Pro Bowl for the fourth time

**2006** Tied for fourth in the NFL with 24 touchdown passes

**2005** Named *Sports Illustrated*'s Sportsman of the Year
Named to the Pro Bowl for the third time
Threw his 100th career regular season touchdown pass

**2004** Won the Super Bowl title for the third time
Was named to the Pro Bowl

**2003** Won the Super Bowl title and the game's MVP award for the
second time

**2002** Led NFL quarterbacks with 28 touchdown passes
Won the Super Bowl title and was named the game's MVP

**2001** Completed the most passes of any Patriot in team history
Named to the Pro Bowl in his first season as a starter

**1999** All-Big Ten Conference second-team selection

**1998** Selected to the All-Big Ten Conference honorable mention
Named to the All-Big Ten Academic team

# Glossary

**conference:** a group of sports teams that play against one another

**division:** within the NFL, one of four sets of teams in each conference. The Patriots are part of the Eastern Division of the American Football Conference.

**draft:** a yearly event in which all professional teams in a sport are given the chance to pick new players from a selected group. Most of the players in the group have played their sport in college.

**kickoff:** a kick that puts the ball into play

**overtime:** in NFL rules, an extra 15 minutes played when the teams are tied. The first team to score wins.

**playbook:** a book that describes plays a team will use in games

**playoffs:** a series of contests played after the regular season has ended

**Pro Bowl:** a game played after each season between the stars of the American Football Conference and the National Football Conference

**punt:** to kick the ball after it is dropped before it hits the ground. A punt results in the opposing team getting control of the ball.

**quarterback:** in football, the person who throws or hands off the ball

**regular season:** the regular schedule for a season. In the NFL, each team plays 16 games. The top 12 teams go to the playoffs.

**rookie:** a player who is playing his or her first season

**running back:** a player whose main job is to run with the ball

**scholarship:** money awarded to a student to pay for the cost of attending college

**snap:** to start a football play by handing or tossing the ball to a quarterback or running back

**third-string:** the name given to the third player at a certain position. The first-string player is the starting player. The second-string player would replace the first-string player and so on.

**veteran:** a player who has played for a number of years

# Further Reading & Websites

Bowker, Paul. *Playing Pro Football*. Minneapolis: Lerner Publications, 2015.

Kennedy, Mike, and Mark Stewart. *Touchdown: The Power and Precision of Football's Perfect Play*. Minneapolis: Millbrook Press, 2010.

New England Patriots
http://www.patriots.com
Check out the official website of the New England Patriots.

Official NFL Site
http://www.nfl.com
The official National Football League website provides fans with game action, biographies of players, and information about football.

Savage, Jeff. *Peyton Manning*. Minneapolis: Lerner Publications, 2013.

*Sports Illustrated Kids*
http://www.sikids.com
The *Sports Illustrated Kids* website covers all sports, including football.

**LERNER**

**SOURCE**

Expand learning beyond the printed book.  Download free, complementary educational resources for this book from our website, www.lerneresource.com.

# Index

Belichick, Bill, 8, 17

Bledsoe, Drew, 16–17, 24

Brady, Galynn, 11, 23

Brady, Tom: and baseball, 12–13;
  career highlights, 29; childhood,
  11–12; college career, 14–15; family
  of, 11; high school career, 12–13;
  NFL career, 16–17, 18–22, 23–28

Brady, Tom, Sr., 11

Bündchen, Gisele, 25–26

Carr, Lloyd, 14

Disney World, 23

Junipero Serra High School, 12

Montana, Joe, 11

Most Valuable Player (MVP), 9, 22, 23,
  29

New England Patriots, 4–9, 16–17,
  18–22, 23–28

New York Giants, 26–27

NFL draft, 16

Orange Bowl, 15

Pro Bowls, 23, 29

Super Bowls, 8–9, 20–22, 24–27, 29

University of Michigan, 14–15

# Photo Acknowledgments

The images in this book are used with the permission of: AP Photo/Damian Strohmeyer, pp. 4, 5, 8; © Jim Davis/The Boston Globe/Getty Images, pp. 6, 7; © John W. McDonough/Icon SMI, p. 10; Courtesy of Russ Bertetta, Junipero Serra High School, p. 12; © Reuters/CORBIS, pp. 15, 16, 18, 19, 21, 22 (all); AP Photo/Peter Cosgrove, p. 23; AP Photo/Mark J. Terrill, p. 24; AP Photo/ Tim DiPace, p. 25; © Larry Busacca/Getty Images, p. 26; © Rob Tringali/ Sportschrome/Getty Images, p. 27; © Al Pereira/Getty Images, p. 27; © John Tlumacki/The Boston Globe/Getty Images, p. 28; © Mark Cunningham/ Detroit Lions/Getty Images, p. 29.

Front cover:© Scott Cunningham/Getty Images

Main body text set in Caecilia LT Std 55 Roman 16/28.
Typeface provided by Adobe Systems.